D0466229

LOOK!
WHAT DO YOU SEE?

An **ART PUZZLE BOOK** of
American & Chinese Songs

太隋 XU BING

with illustrations by Becca Stadtlander

WITHDRAWN

VIKING

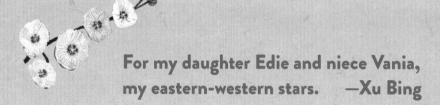

For my daughter Edie and niece Vania,
my eastern-western stars.   —Xu Bing

VIKING
Penguin Young Readers
An imprint of Penguin Random House LLC
375 Hudson Street
New York, New York 10014

First published in the United States of America by Viking,
an imprint of Penguin Random House LLC, 2017

Calligraphy copyright © 2017 by Xu Bing

Illustrations copyright © 2017 by Becca Stadtlander

Translations of Chinese songs by John Cayley,
copyright © 2017 Penguin Random House LLC

"Camptown Races" and "Oh Susannah" lyrics by Stephen Foster
"When Johnny Comes Marching Home Again" lyrics by John Gilmore
"This Land Is Your Land" lyrics by Woody Guthrie
"Take Me Out to the Ball Game" lyrics by Jack Norworth
"America the Beautiful" lyrics by Katherine Lee Bates
"Home on the Range" lyrics by John A. Lomax

Penguin supports copyright. Copyright fuels creativity, encourages
diverse voices, promotes free speech, and creates a vibrant culture.
Thank you for buying an authorized edition of this book and for complying
with copyright laws by not reproducing, scanning, or distributing any part
of it in any form without permission. You are supporting writers and
allowing Penguin to continue to publish books for every reader.

LIBRARY OF CONGRESS CATALOGING-IN-PUBLICATION DATA
Names: Xu, Bing, 1955– author. | Stadtlander, Becca, illustrator.
Title: Look! what do you see? : an art puzzle book of American
and Chinese songs / by Xu Bing ; with illustrations by Becca
Stadtlander.
Description: New York : Viking Books for Young Readers, 2017. |
Includes bibliographical references and index. | Audience: Ages 7
up. | Audience: Grades 4 to 6. |
Identifiers: LCCN 2017005432 (print) |
LCCN 2017013218 (ebook) | ISBN
9780698186392 () | ISBN 9780698186378 () | ISBN
9780698186385 ( ) | ISBN
9780451473776 (hardback)
Subjects: LCSH: Picture puzzles—Juvenile literature. | Visual
perception—Juvenile literature. | Word games—Juvenile literature. |
BISAC: JUVENILE NONFICTION / Art / General. | JUVENILE
NONFICTION / Music / General. | JUVENILE NONFICTION
/ People & Places / United States / General.
Classification: LCC GV1507.P47 (ebook) | LCC GV1507.P47 X8
2017 (print) | DDC
793.73—dc23
LC record available at https://lccn.loc.gov/2017005432

Manufactured in China   Book design by Jim Hoover
This book is set in Goudy Old Style and Brandon Grotesque

10 9 8 7 6 5 4 3 2 1

TOP SECRET ASSIGNMENT

TO:

The world's top mystery solvers, puzzle masters, and cryptographers.

YOUR MISSION:

This book is written entirely in secret code, and we need you to crack it. The code is called Square Word Calligraphy, and it was invented in 1994 by Xu Bing, an internationally famous contemporary artist. It's not an easy code, and it's probably not one you've ever seen before. But if anyone can figure it out, it's you.

A CLUE:

We have studied these pages and determined that the first twelve spreads in here are classic American songs. Maybe you know them from campfire or school bus sing-alongs. The last five spreads are translations of classic Chinese songs. If you are from China, you might know these from camp or school sing-alongs, too.

We're counting on you to decipher the text and discover its meaning. Just remember: the closer you look, the more you can see. Now, begin!

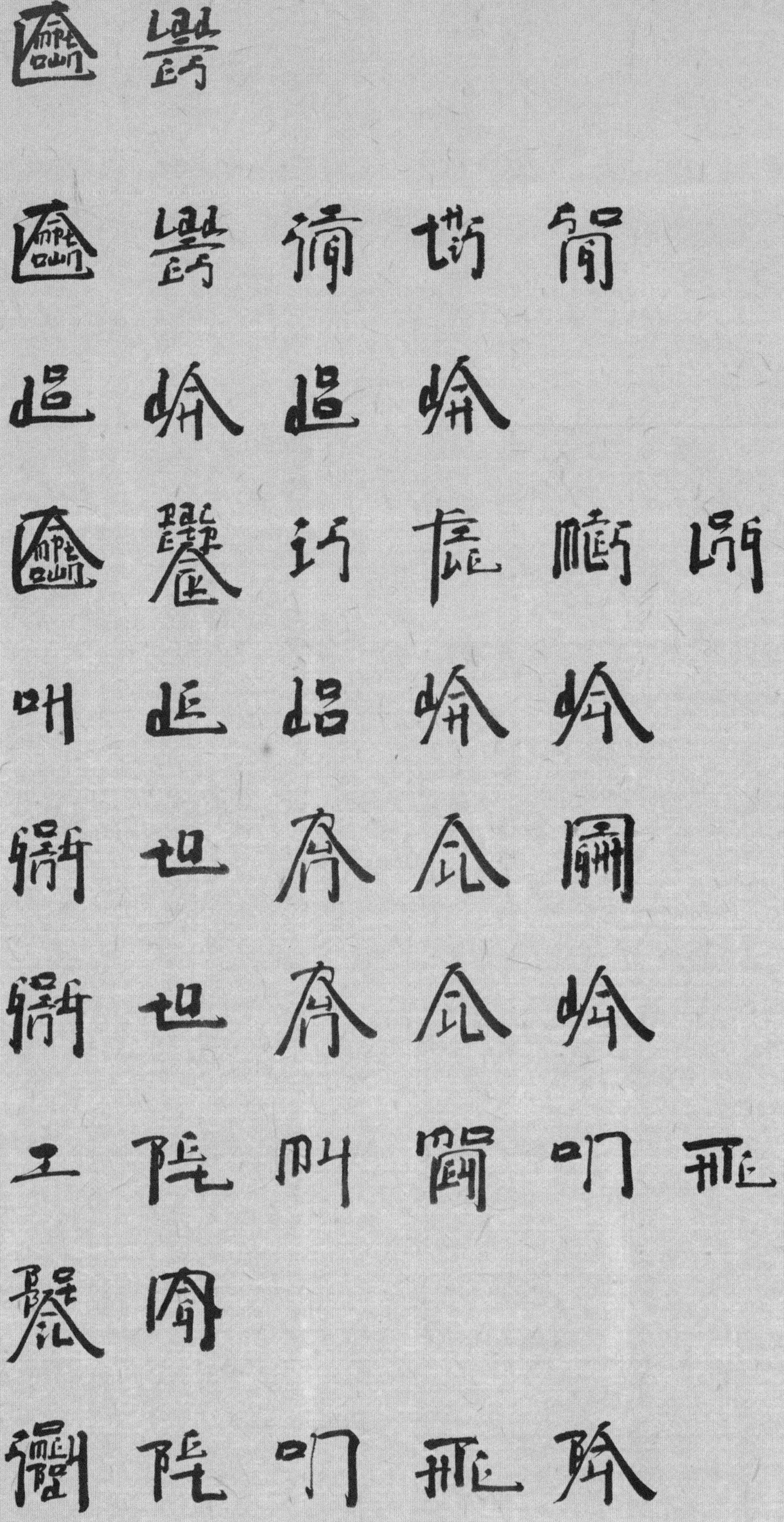

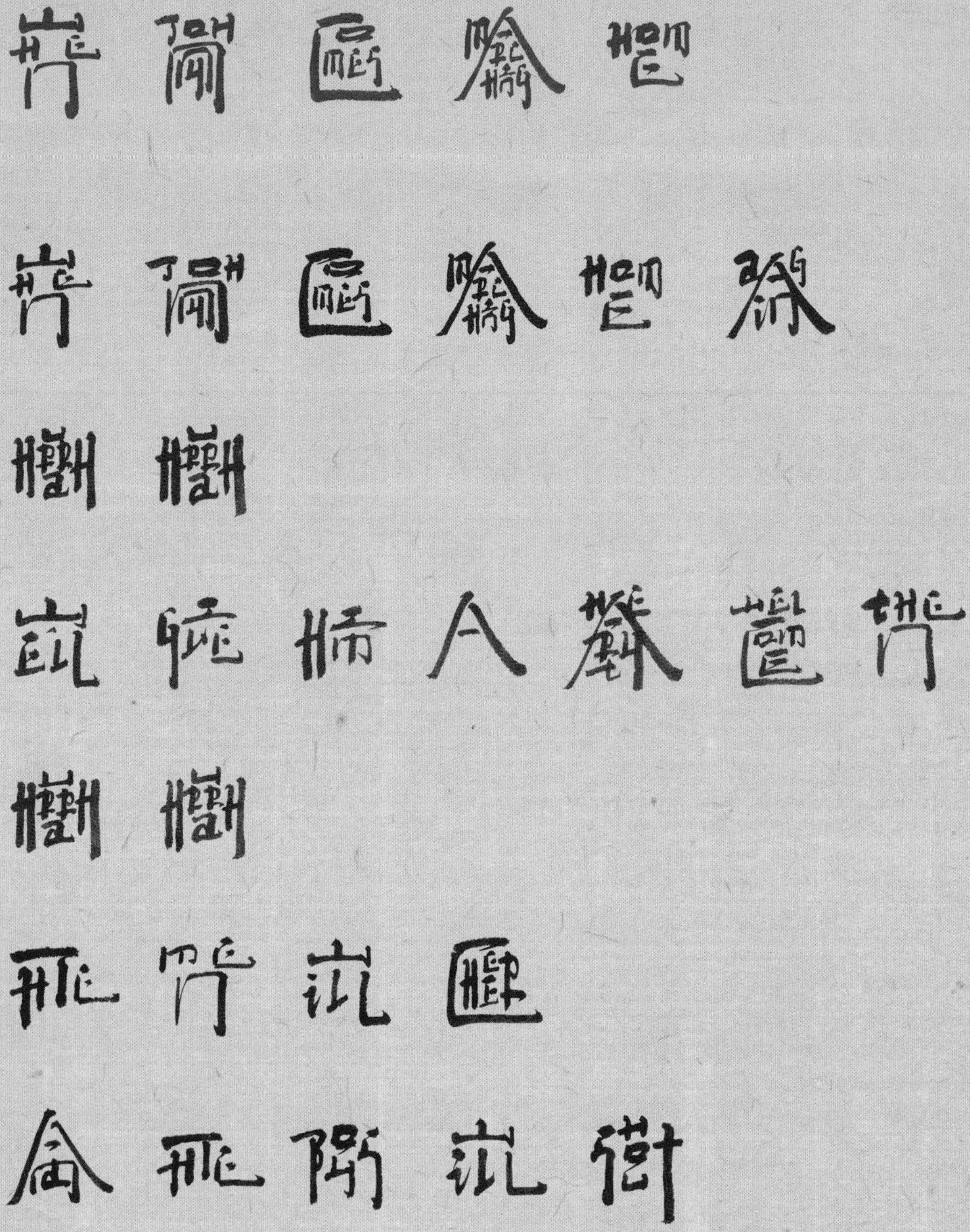

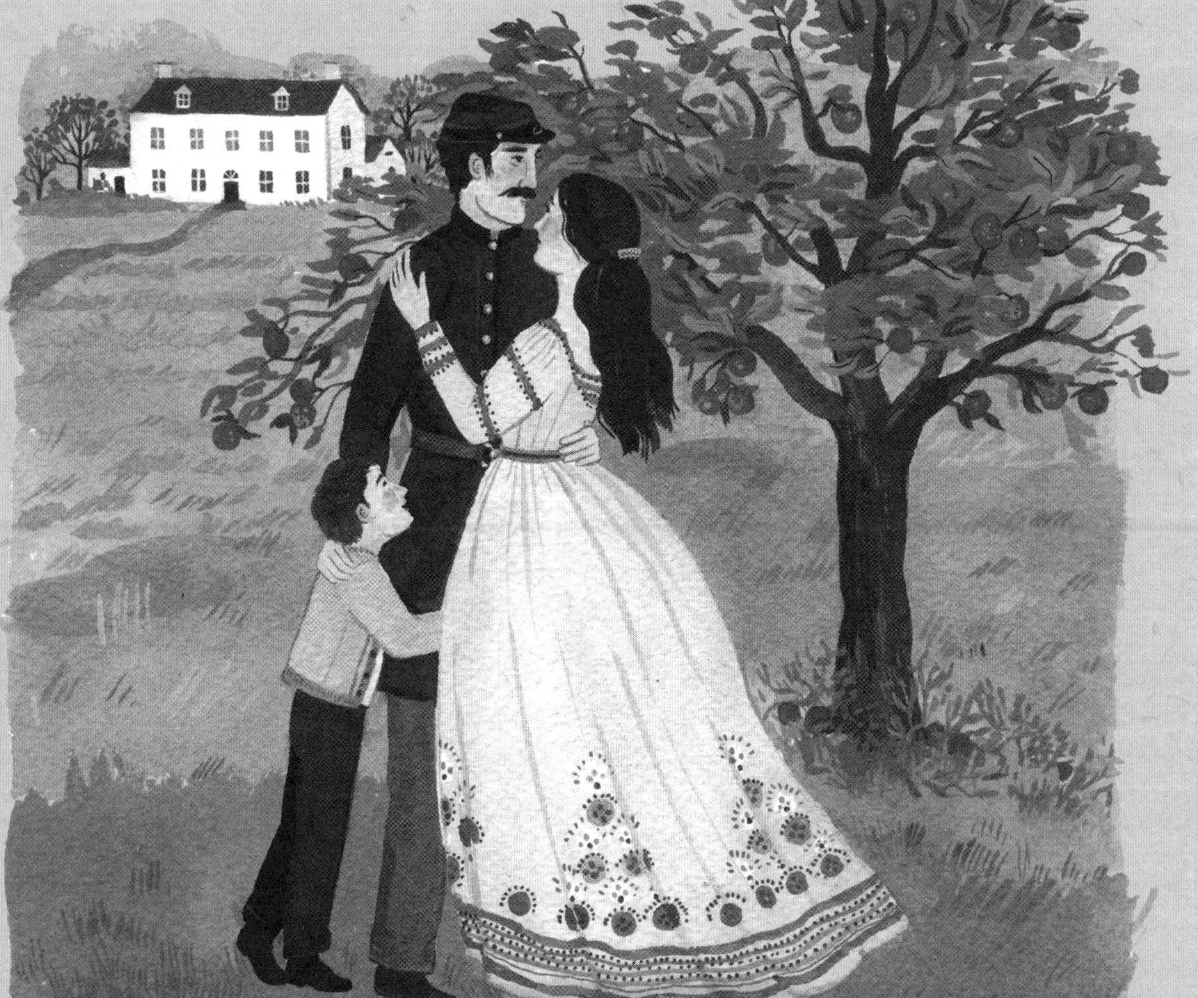

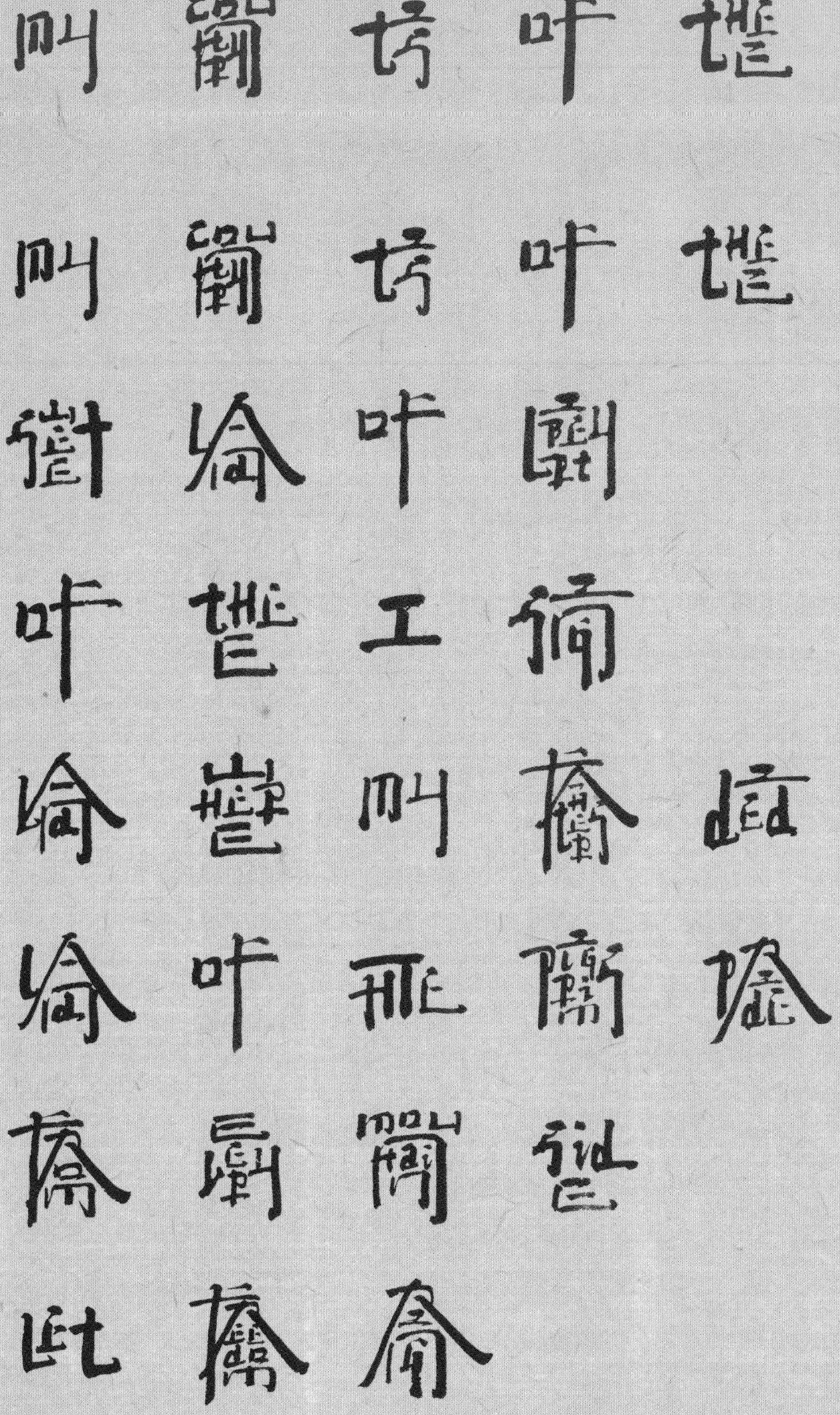

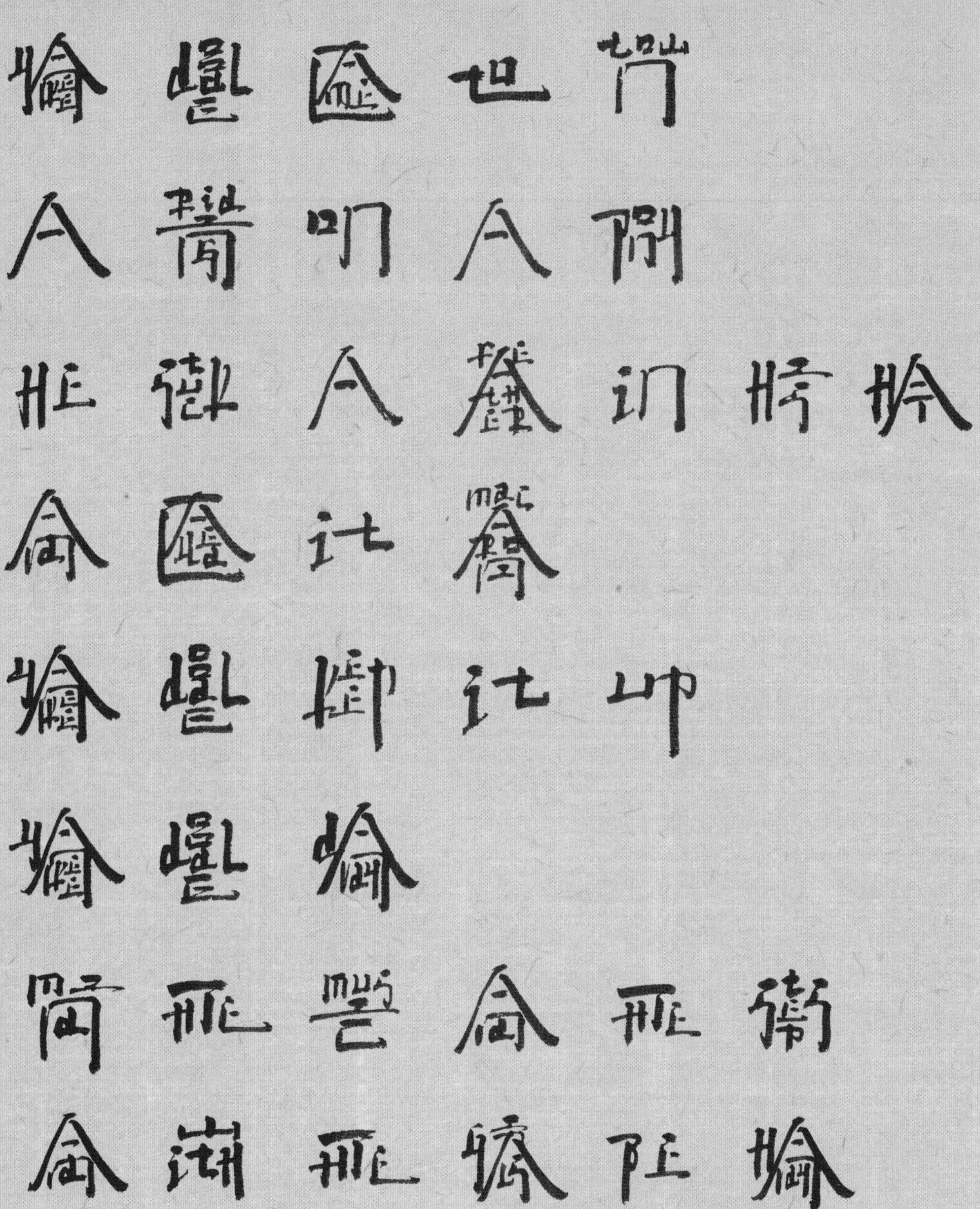

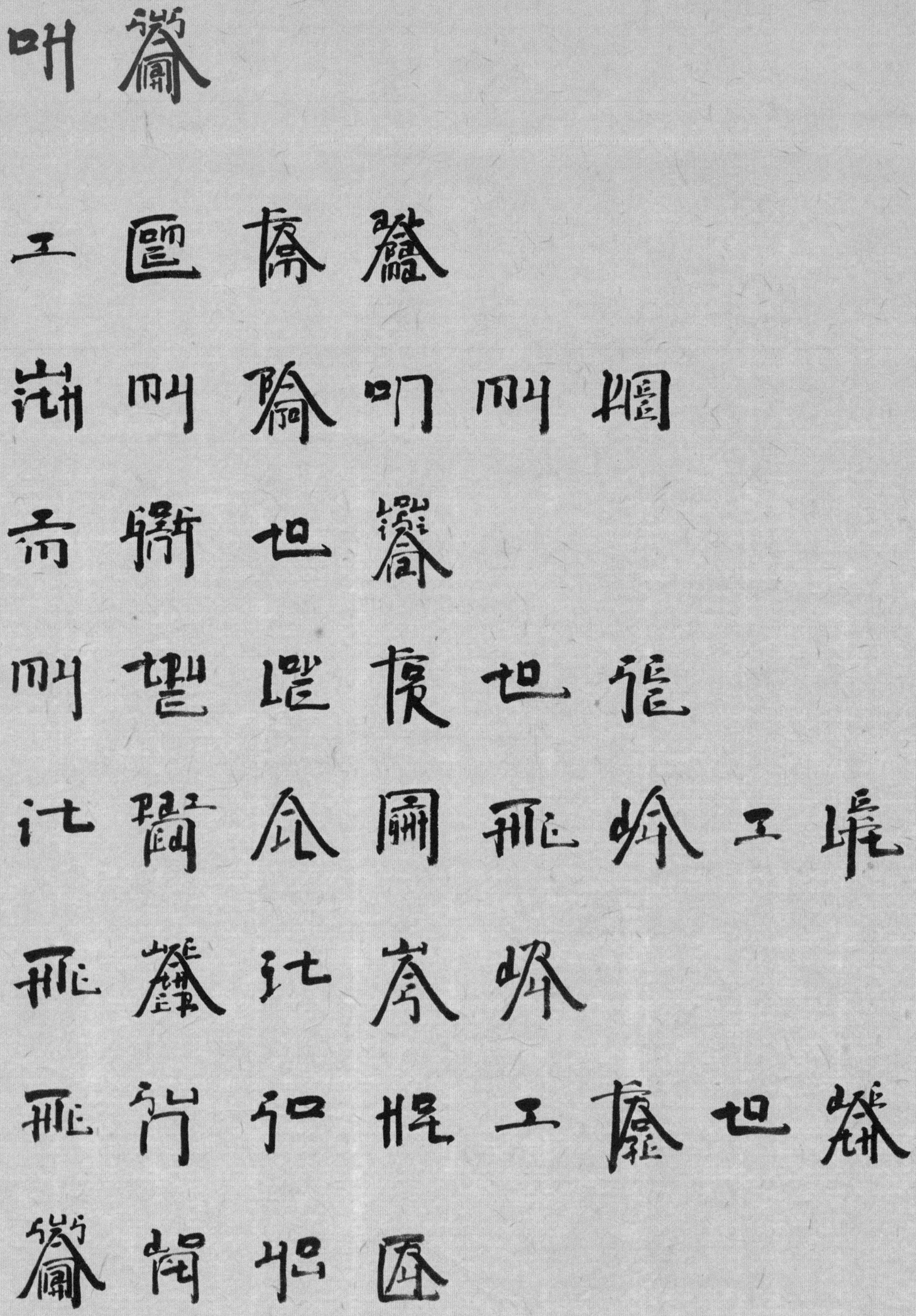

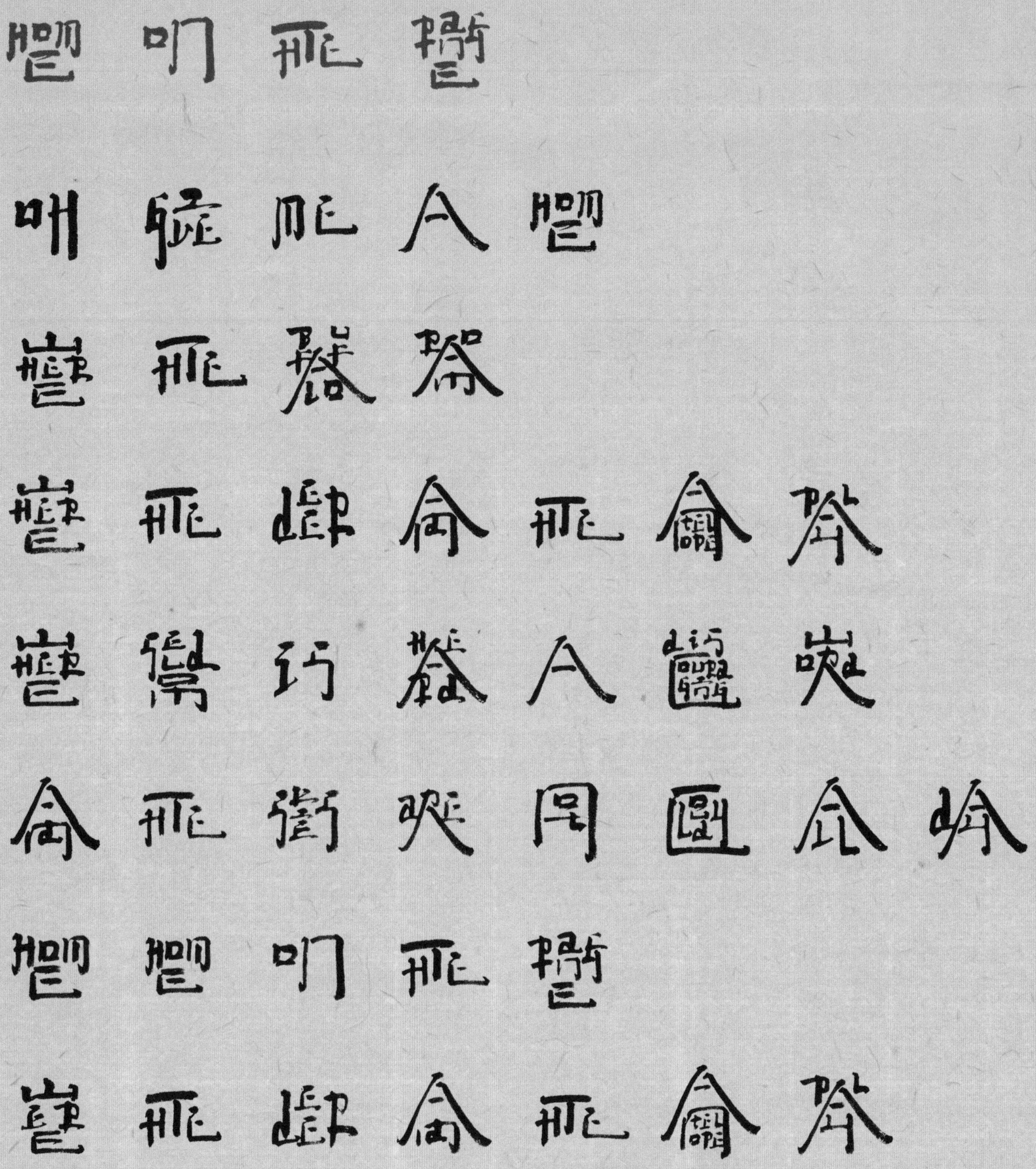

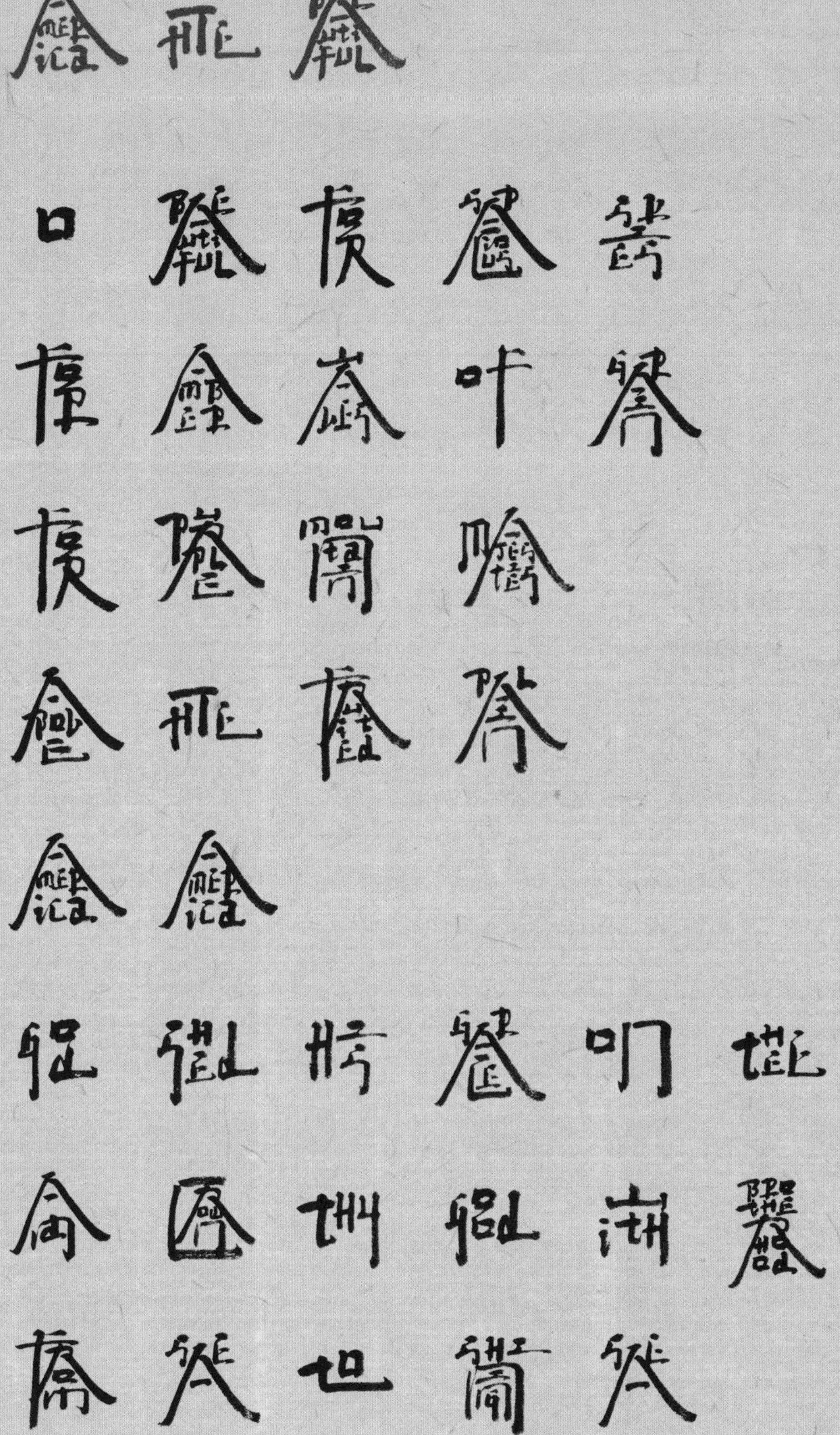

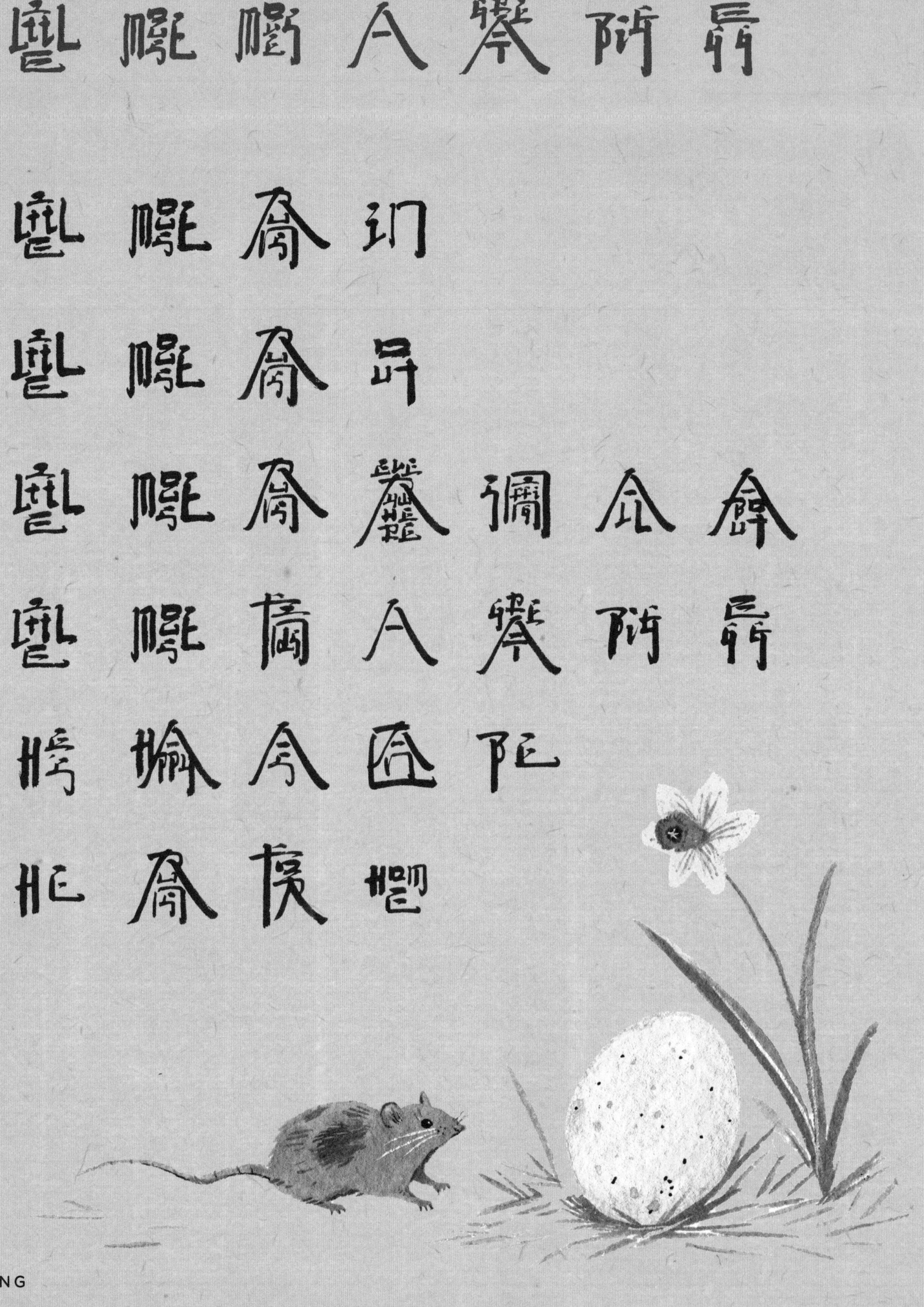

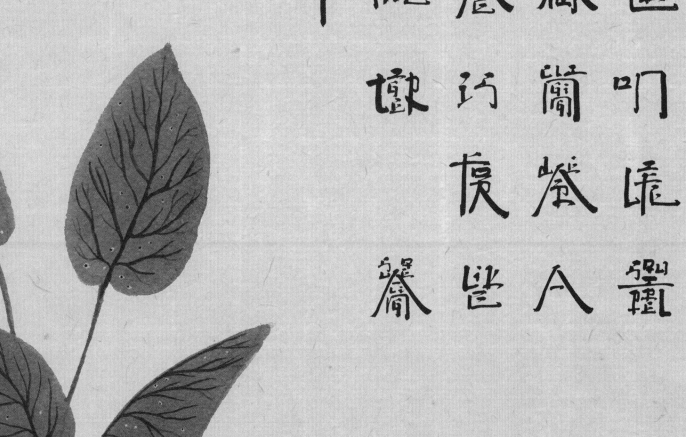

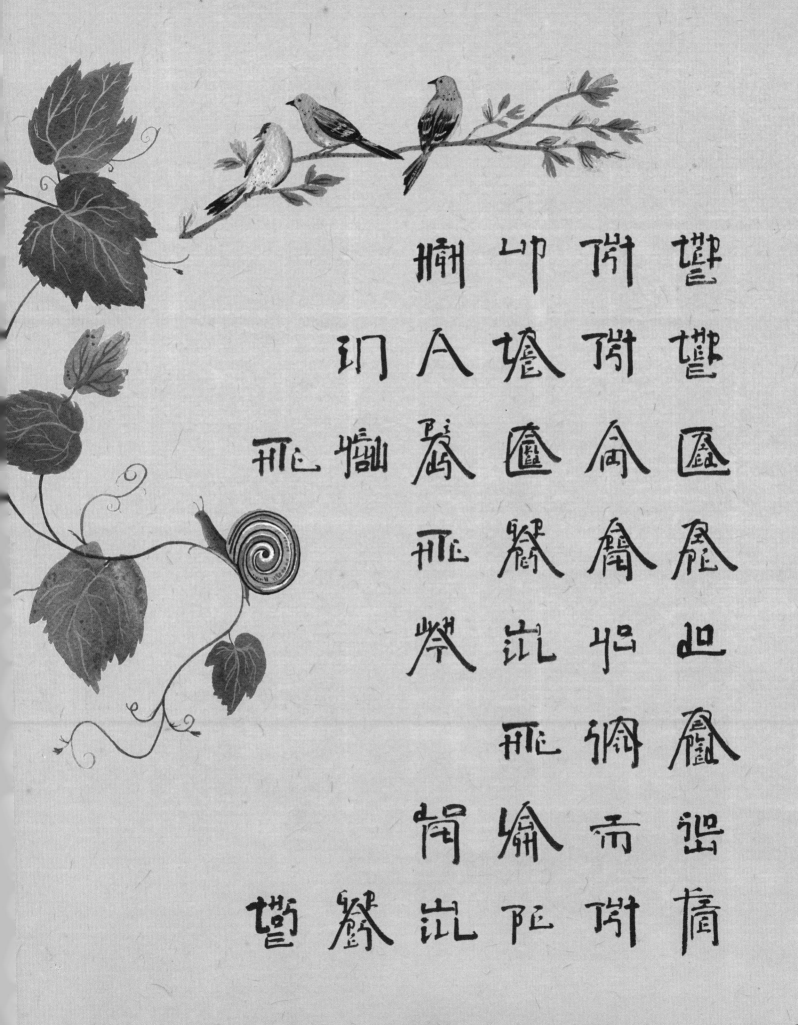

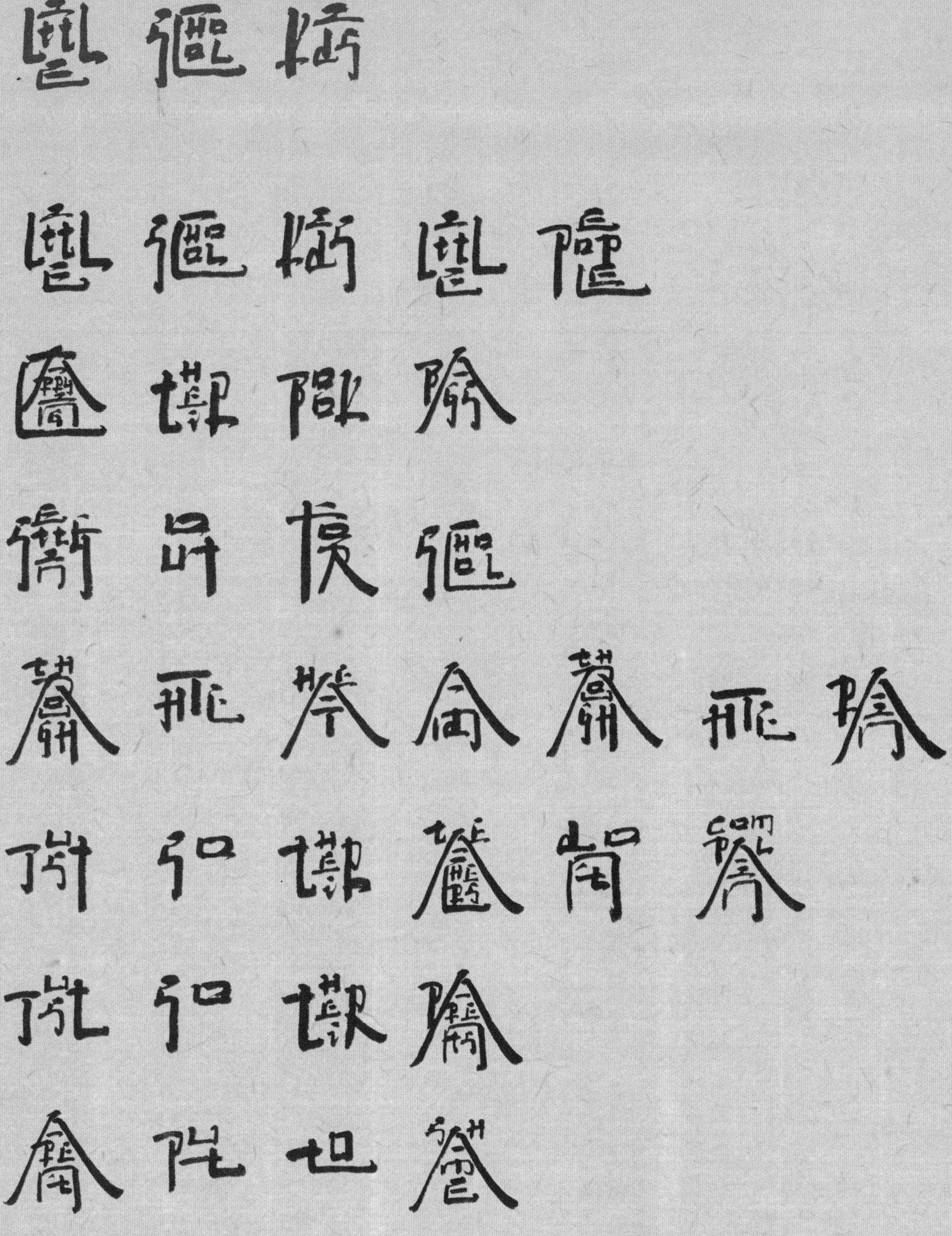

Table of Square Word Elements

	F	M	T
	G	N	U
A	H	O	V
B	I	P	W
C	J	Q	X
D	K	R	Y
E	L	S	Z

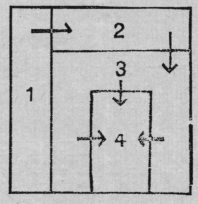

1. From left to right
2. From top to bottom
3. From outside to inside

ANSWER KEY

p. 2–3: Skip to My Lou: Skip, skip, skip to my Lou, / Skip to my Lou, my darling. / There's a little red wagon, / Paint it blue. / Skip to my Lou, my darling.

p. 4–5: Dear Liza: There's a hole in the bucket, / Dear Liza, dear Liza, / There's a hole in the bucket, / Dear Liza, a hole. / Then fix it, dear Henry /Dear Henry, dear Henry, / Then fix it, dear Henry / Dear Henry, fix the hole.

p. 6–7: Camptown Ladies: Camptown ladies sing this song, / Doo-dah, doo-dah. / Camptown race-track is five miles long, / Oh, de doo-dah day. / Going to run all night, / Going to run all day. / I bet my money on the bobtail nag. / Somebody bet on the bay.

p. 8–9: When Johnny Comes Marching Home: When Johnny comes marching home again, / Hurrah! Hurrah! / We'll give him a hearty welcome then, / Hurrah! Hurrah! / The men will cheer / And the boys will shout. / The ladies they will all turn out. / And we'll all feel gay / When Johnny comes marching home.

p. 10–11: This Land Is Your Land: This land is your land, / This land is my land, / From California / To the New York island, / From the redwood forest / To the Gulf Stream waters, / This land was made for you and me.

p. 12–13: Take Me Out to the Ball Game: Take me out to the ball game, / Take me out with the crowd; / Buy me some peanuts and Cracker Jack. / I don't care if I never get back. / Let me root, root, root / For the home team, / If they don't win, it's a shame. / For it's one, two, three strikes, you're out, / At the old ball game.

p. 14–15: My Country 'Tis of Thee: My country, 'tis of thee, / Sweet land of liberty, / Of thee I sing; / Land where my fathers died, / Land of the pilgrims' pride, / From every mountain side / Let freedom ring.

p. 16–17: Yankee Doodle Came to Town: Yankee Doodle came to town, / A-riding on a pony; / He stuck a feather in his hat / And called it macaroni. / Yankee Doodle keep it up, / Yankee Doodle dandy; / Mind the music and the steps / And with the girls be handy.

p. 18–19: I've Been Working on the Railroad: I've been working on the railroad / All the live-long day. / I've been working on the railroad / Just to pass the time away. / Don't you hear the whistle blowing, / Rise up so early in the morn; / Don't you hear the captain shouting, / "Dinah, blow your horn!" / Dinah, won't you blow, / Dinah, won't you blow, / Dinah, won't you blow your horn?

p. 20–21: Oh Susannah: I come from Alabama / With my banjo on my knee. / I'm going to Louisiana / My true love for to see. / It rained all night the day I left, / The weather it was dry, / The sun so hot I froze to death— / Susannah, don't you cry. / Oh! Susannah, / Oh don't you cry for me, / For I come from Alabama / With my banjo on my knee.

p. 22–23: Home on the Range: Oh, give me a home / Where the buffalo roam, / Where the deer and the antelope play. / Where seldom is heard a discouraging word, / And the skies are not cloudy all day. / Home, home on the range, / Where the deer and the antelope play. / Where seldom is heard a discouraging word, / And the skies are not cloudy all day.

p. 24–25: America the Beautiful: O beautiful for spacious skies, / For amber waves of grain, / For purple mountain majesties / Above the fruited plain! / America! America! / God shed his grace on thee / And crown thy good with brotherhood / From sea to shining sea!

p. 26–27: Little Mouse Moves a Great Big Egg: Little Mouse runs in. / Little Mouse runs out. / Little Mouse runs everywhere, sniffing all about. / Little Mouse finds a Great Big Egg: / He's happy as can be! / He runs for home / But bumps right into Great Big Mouse. / Little Mouse's eyes light up: / He's got a Big Idea. / He wraps his paws around the egg, / Yells, "Grab my tail and run for home!"

p. 28–29: When Little White Rabbit Built His House: When Little White Rabbit built his house, / The dog and the monkey came to help. / Fetching this and fetching that, / Lifting this and lifting that, / And soon enough / They'd built themselves / A pretty little house. / But once inside, it's black as tar. / Who left the windows out!?

p. 30–31: Tiger Learns to Climb: Little Squirrel is Tiger's teacher. / She teaches Tiger what, exactly? / She teaches Tiger trees. / Tiger learns his lesson: / How to climb. / But getting down / He's quite forgot. / The problem is that he is / Up the tree and stuck. / Tiger is clinging on / For dear life, / Squealing like a squirrel!

p. 32–33: The Snail and the Yellow Birds: Just outside the gate, / Just outside in front, / There grew a lovely grape vine. / Down below, a tiny snail was climbing, / Inch by inch, toward the grapes. / High up just there, / In a tree just there, / The yellow birds cackled and cried, / "The grapes aren't ripe! / What will you do?" / The snail replied, / "Don't laugh! I'm slow. / Those grapes will be just fine!"

p. 34–35: Little School Kids: Little school kids, little people / Carrying their book bags, / Setting out for school / Through the heat and through the rain, / Just so their teachers don't complain, / Just so their parents / Aren't put to shame. / Little school kids, little people / Carrying their book bags, / Setting out for school / Not for riches, not for fame, / Just so they can change their lives. / Just so they can reach the skies.